Gardening
in retirement

D0278880

Cover: a patio can be a comfortable and attractive extra "living room" (photograph by Michael Warren)

Overleaf: dwarf rhododendrons make a colourful splash in a raised bed

Gardening
in retirement

A Wisley handbook

Alec Bristow

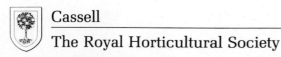

Cassell

The Royal Horticultural Society

Cassell Educational Limited
Artillery House, Artillery Row
London SW1 1RT
for the Royal Horticultural Society

First published 1988

British Library Cataloguing in Publication Data

Bristow, Alec
    Gardening in retirement. — (Wisley handbooks).
    1. Gardening – For old persons
    I. Title   II. Royal Horticultural Society
    III. Series
    635′,024056

    ISBN 0-304-31142-1

Photographs by Alec Bristow and Michael Warren
Design by Lesley Stewart
Phototypesetting by Chapterhouse Ltd, Formby
Printed in Hong Kong by Wing King Tong Co. Ltd

Contents

Introduction

Of all the activities to which retired people can devote their increased leisure, gardening is among the most satisfying, and the pleasures it brings, if perhaps gentler than those of youth, can be deeper and more lasting. Many people whose youthful ambition was to conquer the world find, as they reach their later years, that there is greater reward in achieving the more realistic goal of managing a garden successfully.

Though most people, when they retire, can look forward to many years of unimpaired physical vigour, sooner or later that vigour will begin to decline and tasks which were once easy may become harder and take longer. For this reason, it is best to start planning the garden for retirement as early as possible and, in particular, to complete the heavy constructional jobs which require physical strength before they become too much of a burden. The aim is not to eliminate work entirely – that would not only be impossible, but would rob gardening of much of its pleasure, most of its purpose and all of its sense of achievement – but to make the tasks that remain as effort-free and enjoyable as possible.

Opposite: low-maintenance gardening, with dwarf conifers, alpines and container plants
Below: a window box bright with geraniums

Design for retirement

For various reasons, many people decide to move to a new house when they are nearing retirement, which often means creating a new garden from scratch. It may cause a pang or two to leave the old garden and part with some of your favourite plants, particularly those you have planted yourself and watched with pleasure and pride over the years. In some cases, you might be able to transfer them to the new garden, by taking seed, cuttings or divisions. This, however, is not always possible, either because the plant is difficult to propagate or because it is unsuitable for the new conditions. For instance, lime-haters such as camellias and rhododendrons, which may thrive in the acid conditions of the old garden, would not take kindly to a new site with chalky soil. The best way to avoid such mistakes is to note what kinds of plants do well in the neighbourhood to which you are moving. It is a good plan to visit local garden centres and see what their best-selling lines are; they would soon lose their customers if what they stocked was unsuitable for the district.

There are, in any case, two excellent reasons why it may be wise *not* to take too many old faithfuls with you to your new garden. First, changing your surroundings encourages you to look forward to the future and gives a perfect opportunity to make the acquaintance of unfamiliar plants. Secondly, breeders compete all the time to produce novelties, in an attempt to improve on what has gone before. So you may well find that the current choice of cultivars and selections far surpasses – in such characteristics as beauty, vigour, hardiness and resistance to pests and diseases – those now outdated ones which were the very latest thing when you first bought them many years ago.

Many people may not be able to, or may not wish to, uproot themselves and move to a new place. For them, the question is what modifications are necessary to make the present garden a more desirable place for retirement. The same general considerations apply, however, whether you are planning to alter an old garden or create a new one.

Since the design of a garden is determined by such factors as the size, shape, position, contour and aspect of the site, the purpose to which it is to be put, the nature of the soil and the likes and dislikes of the owner, there can be no such thing as a standard garden plan. The best approach is to study what other people have done

A terracotta pot attractively planted with ornamental cabbage, geranium, petunia and busy lizzy

and see what features of their designs you can borrow, adapt and combine to suit your own tastes, requirements and conditions. A great many ideas can be picked up from visiting other gardens, from illustrated articles in magazines and from the wide range of books available on garden design. (See also the Wisley handbooks, *Plans for small gardens* and *Plans for small gardens 2*).

The overriding consideration when planning a garden for retirement is to arrange all its elements so that the amount of work needed to maintain it in good condition is reduced to the minimum and, if possible, diminishes as time goes by. The tasks which take the most time and effort in an average garden include weeding, mowing, digging, clipping, staking, pruning and watering and, in the following pages, some ways of cutting down the time and energy they demand will be suggested. At the onset, however, good design, thorough preparation, careful construction and suitable choice of plants will all help to achieve the ideal.

DRAWING A PLAN

The first rule is this: a little mental effort initially can save a great deal of physical effort later on. A plan of the site drawn to scale is the starting point for any successful garden design and your most important labour-saving tools are paper, pencil and a good piece of india-rubber. Mistakes made on paper are easily rubbed out and put right, but mistakes made on the site itself can take a lot of hard work to correct – and may remain with you for ever, causing a great deal of unnecessary work later on.

If the property is a new one, perhaps part of a recently built residential estate, a plan of the site should be available, but the scale is not likely to be large enough nor the site measurements accurate enough to be useful. So you must take your own measurements and draw your own plan. Start with the outline of the house and use this as a base to measure the boundaries of the plot and the position of fixed things like manhole covers, together with existing features you intend to preserve, such as a tree (though it must be said that, on a new residential estate occupying what used to be agricultural land, any trees left by the builder, such as common species of oak, beech or lime, will probably be much too big for most gardens). Then transfer this information to paper, making the drawing to as large a scale as possible, so that there is plenty of room to mark in everything you want in your garden. It is a much easier job if you use a sheet of squared graph paper, each square representing a square foot (or, keeping up with present-day trends, you may prefer to work in metres and centimetres). If the ground has a marked slope or pronounced humps and hollows, levels should be taken in several places (see p. 21) and noted down at appropriate points on the plan. This is in preparation for altering the contour of the ground, in order to achieve a satisfactory design and make the garden easier to maintain – and safer too. (For dealing with a sloping site, see p. 23.)

A scale drawing of the site gives you an overall view of its shape and proportions and a basis on which to design the garden. The main features, such as flower beds, borders, vegetable patch, hedges, lawn, patio, path and steps, should be pencilled in and can then be altered or eliminated if necessary. When it comes to the choice of plants, specimen trees or shrubs can be correctly spaced on paper to prevent overcrowding once they have grown to their full size in the garden.

Opposite above: deep borders should be accessible from both sides
Below: a patio is one of the most valuable features of a garden planned for retirement

PRACTICAL CONSIDERATIONS

Numerous practical considerations enter into any garden design and even more so one which is planned for retirement. Think carefully before you sketch in the lawn, for instance. Are you prepared for the mowing and general maintenance it will require, or would it be better to pave the area over? The same applies to a vegetable plot or greenhouse, both of which could demand more energy than you are willing to give in future years. A hedge may be a more effective means of shelter and more attractive than a fence, but it will need regular clipping. Keep to simple lines and shapes when drafting beds, paths and especially the lawn and make sure that the flower borders are narrow enough to reach and tend easily. Raised beds or, on a sloping site, retaining walls are conducive to more comfortable gardening and could be worth incorporating into the design, particularly as they involve some construction work. Although the actual planting will come later, trees should be included at this stage, whether existing or proposed. Their presence makes a garden complete, adding height and focus and providing valuable shade and shelter, but they need careful selection and placing.

One factor of crucial importance in any layout is that of access, not only between different parts of the garden but from the house to the garden; if that is not made as smooth and trouble-free as possible, none of the other elements in the design can do much to remedy matters. Paths should be wide enough for two people to walk abreast, allowing ample space for a wheelbarrow or, if necessary, a wheelchair. There should be no overhanging branches, for these can be a real menace to users of the path, particularly if their eyesight is not too good. Fallen leaves can be a hazard too if they are allowed to remain on the path and become wet and slippery. More dangerous still, especially on shady paths, is the slimy film of green algae which is likely to form on surfaces that remain damp for prolonged periods and which tends to reappear rapidly, even after being treated with one of the algicides sold for the purpose.

Doors from the house must be easy to open and wide enough to cause no problems (in the possible future, if not at present) with a wheelchair or walking frame. It is desirable that the adjoining terrace or patio to which the door gives access should be on the same level as the floor of the house, to avoid tripping and make it easier to take a tea trolley or wheelchair outside. The terrace may be looked upon as an extension of the house, designed for ease

Opposite: a patch of grass and a swing may be helpful for entertaining young visitors

and comfort. It should be sheltered and sunny and large enough for a chair or two and maybe a small table, so that on fine days you can sit outside, alone or with friends, enjoying a breath of fresh air without having to move more than a few steps from the house.

Such things as the compost bin, clothes line and tool shed are often relegated to the far end of the garden, but it is much more sensible to have them near the house, along with the dustbin. If these utilitarian, but not very pretty, objects can be grouped together unobtrusively and reached through a side door, there is no point in trying to camouflage them. If, however, they have to be sited where their appearance might spoil the effect, they can be hidden from view by some form of screen with a climber or two trained up it.

One thing that should not be overlooked is the question of visitors. Well-behaved adults will not need any special provision made for them, but if you expect energetic young grandchildren, they should have somewhere in the garden to play, with perhaps a swing or a slide which can be dismantled and stowed away when not in use. Needless to say, any play area – even just a patch of grass (which should be of a hard-wearing kind) where a ball can be kicked around – ought to be sited well away from particularly valuable or delicate plants. Nothing can be more fraying to the nerves and temper than to be in a constant state of anxiety about possible damage. A garden, especially in one's more contemplative years, should be a place of peace and tranquillity, not a place where you find yourself continually nagging your young visitors or, perhaps worse still, bottling up your feelings and pretending not to mind about your precious plants, in case you should be thought an old fusspot.

Because, when you retire, your life ceases to be ruled to the same extent by the clock, you will probably find yourself tending to remain in bed longer and stay indoors more, particularly on cold or rainy days. By careful choice and placing of plants, it should always be possible to look out of the window and see something attractive in the garden.

To sum up, a garden designed for retirement should be easy to get to from the house and to navigate safely, should need as little maintenance as possible and should always look inviting both from the inside and the outside.

Construction work

After the layout of the garden has been planned to your satisfaction, the heavy constructional tasks will need to be tackled; the sooner these are over and done with the better. If you can afford it, you may prefer to get the work, or at any rate the heaviest jobs, done by a contractor. On the other hand, if you feel strong and energetic enough to tackle it yourself, with help perhaps from family and friends, you can save a considerable amount of money, besides being able to take personal pride in the result.

In either case, the most important principle is to let the first expense be the last. That applies not only to expense in monetary terms but even more to expense in terms of effort. The falsest of all false economies is to use cheap materials or skimp the job and find yourself paying for it later in unnecessary work and extra bills for repairs or reconstruction.

PATHS

For ease of use, paths should be at least 4 ft (120 cm) wide. They should always be laid on clean weed-free ground and should have a good foundation for stability and drainage. A path, or just a paved edging, is a useful labour-saving device for the margins of a lawn. Sunk slightly below the level of the turf, it allows the grass to

A neat brick edging to a lawn saves labour

be mown right to the verge, so that the edges do not have to be clipped. Similarly, it is much easier to keep the front of a border tidy if it adjoins a path rather than a lawn, which requires constant trimming to prevent the grass encroaching. For the less mobile, a path may be essential to provide access to the border.

The choice of material is of great importance, as is the way the path is laid. It is vital that it should have an absolutely firm non-slip surface. Though gravel may be one of the cheapest materials and very attractive when well looked after, its tendency to cause skidding can make it one of the most dangerous. It also demands the drudgery of continual weeding, mending and rolling.

Concrete

The most trouble-free path is one made of concrete, which should last for the foreseeable future. First, a firm foundation must be made. After marking out the sides of the path with pegs and cord, remove the soil between them to a depth of 9 in. (23 cm); if it is good topsoil, it can be added to the beds and borders. Fill the bottom 6 in. (15 cm) with hard rubble, such as broken bricks or stones, and ram it down. Next, take two wooden planks or boards, $\frac{1}{2}$ or $\frac{3}{4}$ in. (1.3–2 cm) thick and 3 in. (7.5 cm) wide, lay them on edge along the rubble, one on each side of the excavation, and peg them. With a spirit-level, make sure that the top edges of the planks are level along their entire length and also level with each other.

Then prepare the concrete. It can either be made, by mixing one part of cement, two of sand and three of shingle with enough water to form a paste that is easy to spread but not sloppy; or it can be bought ready-mixed, which needs only the addition of water. Spread a layer of concrete 3 in. (7.5 cm) deep between the planks. Finish by smoothing the surface, using a piece of board placed on edge across the wooden planks and drawing it from one end of the section to the other. Be careful not leave any air holes in the concrete. At the end of the section fix a cross-piece of wood the same width as the path and level with the side-pieces. Bring the concrete flush with this; any surplus can be thrown into the foundation of the next section. Cover the surface of the concrete with sacking or plastic sheeting to stop it drying too quickly, for the longer it takes, the stronger it will be. In two or three days, when the concrete has set, the wooden planks can be moved forward and the next section of concrete laid in the same way. Make sure that the rear of the new section is laid firmly against the front of the previous one (see figure 1a); if a gap is left between them, it can become invaded with stubborn weeds which are extremely difficult to eradicate.

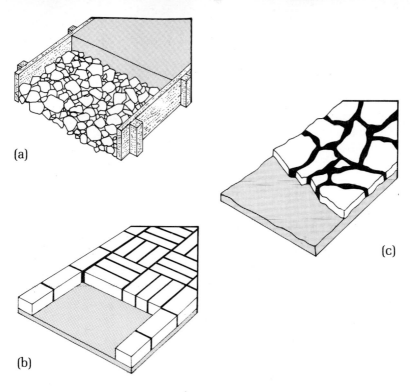

(a)

(b)

(c)

Figure 1: constructing a path – (a) concrete; (b) brick; (c) crazy paving

The colour of ordinary concrete is somewhat dull and can be improved by mixing in a special powder, available in several different colours. However, although concrete is ideal for utilitarian paths in such places as the vegetable garden, many people find its appearance very unprepossessing in the rest of the garden or near the house. More attractive paving materials tend to be more expensive than concrete, but they do not have its cheapening effect. Indeed, they are likely not only to improve the appearance of the property, but to increase its value when it passes to your successors.

Stone

Slabs of natural stone make very handsome paths, particularly in formal gardens. They do, however, have two snags. First, they are expensive, especially if they have to be transported from some distance away. Secondly, they are somewhat irregular in thickness, so it takes time and patience to lay them truly level with each other and really firmly. Irregularities of surface and rocking

17

stones spell danger to people who are not so sure on their feet as they used to be in their younger days.

Precast slabs

These are made of artificial stone in a variety of colours and sizes and can be used in all sorts of different patterns. They may not have quite the distinction of natural stone, but they are cheaper and, being absolutely uniform in thickness, much easier to lay.

Bricks

These can be laid on edge in an almost unlimited range of attractive patterns, including straight, curved and herringbone (see figure 1b). They give great visual richness, by themselves or in combination with other materials like stone or cobbles. They must be of a kind that will not be damaged by frost and they must be laid in such a way that weeds are discouraged from growing between them (see p. 20).

Crazy paving

This is made up of pieces of broken stone, usually about 2 in. (5 cm) thick, arranged in a random manner (see figure 1c). It is very popular for informal effects, particularly for winding paths, and is much cheaper than natural stone. However, unless it is laid with the greatest care and thoroughness, it can be very treacherous to walk on and can also demand constant maintenance later on.

TERRACES AND PATIOS

A terrace or patio can be constructed from any of the materials recommended for paths. Concrete, though cheap and trouble-free, is generally thought to be unattractive for the purpose and natural or artificial stone slabs are the usual choice.

Plants in tubs, urns or large pots make a very agreeable picture on a terrace next to the house. On days when there is no incentive to go outside, they can be enjoyed through the window and during freezing weather they can easily be brought indoors for protection.

Low-growing plants placed at intervals between the stones can also add interest to a patio, as long as they are used with discretion and do not make the area hazardous to negotiate. These must be planned for before starting to lay the paving, so that

There is a choice of materials for paths and terraces: concrete slabs (above left); crazy paving (above right); and bricks (below)

pockets of soil can be provided for them. Particularly suitable are plants that do not mind being trodden on and will reward you by giving off a pleasant scent after being bruised. Among the best are the prostrate thyme, *Thymus serpyllum*, which makes a dense mat of wiry stems with tiny leaves and bears masses of flowers, from white or pink to deep red according to the form, during the summer; and *Mentha requienii*, which becomes a peppermint-scented carpet studded with minute mauve flowers. Dwarf arenaria, dianthus, geranium, phlox and many others are also good between paving stones.

Laying the paving

The first thing to do is to make a firm foundation in the same way as for a path (see p. 16), using rubble left by the builders or buying a load of hardcore. When this layer has been rammed firm, cover it with a good layer of sand, which will make it easier to lay the paving and improve drainage. Smooth the surface of the sand with a trowel or, better still, a plasterer's float. To make sure the surface is level, stand a plank on edge along it and place a spirit-level on top of this; sand can then be scooped away or added as necessary. This will need to be repeated in several places until the whole area to be paved is level.

Arrange the paving stones or bricks on the sand in any pattern that you find pleasing. To make a lasting job, they should then be fixed so that they do not move, using cement mortar made with four parts sand, one part cement and water as required. Starting at one end, lift out the first piece of paving, spread $\frac{1}{2}$ in. (1 cm) of mortar in its place, put back the piece of paving and tap it firmly into position. Continue with the next piece and work your way along the area until it is completed. Do *not* push the slabs or bricks hard up against each other, but leave about $\frac{1}{2}$ in. (1 cm) between them. This makes laying much easier and also enables more mortar to be worked into the gaps. Pockets of soil can be made here and there to accommodate small plants, but all other joints in the paving should be filled with mortar to prevent weeds insinuating themselves. Be sure to wipe away any surplus mortar while still soft with a brush or damp cloth, so as not to spoil the surface.

LEVELLING THE GROUND

There is no way, short of employing outside contractors, in which you can make sloping ground level without considerable effort. The following method does, however, help to reduce that effort to the minimum necessary to do a satisfactory job.

Low-growing thyme is particularly suitable for planting in pockets of paving, although in this case the path looks a bit treacherous

The first task is to find how much the ground slopes and in what directions, using a spirit-level, a plank and some wooden pegs. At the highest point of the site, drive in a peg until its top is 3 in. (7.5 cm) above the ground. A little less than the plank's length down the slope, drive in another peg to a depth sufficient for the plank to be perfectly level when rested on its edge across the two pegs, as shown by the spirit-level placed on the top edge of the plank. Measure the height of the second peg above the ground; the difference between the heights of the two pegs will give you the difference in ground levels. Continue to measure in this way at intervals over the whole area; by this means you will be able to work out what needs to be dug out and what filled in to create the level you want (see figure 2, p. 22).

When shifting earth from one place to another, it is important to remember that in all areas where plants are to be grown – in other words, everywhere except paved areas – the topsoil must still be on top and the subsoil beneath after the job is completed. The

21

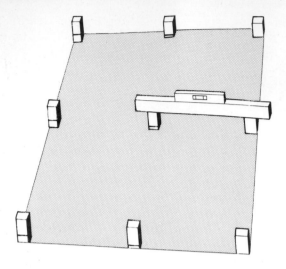

Figure 2: taking levels to find out how much the ground slopes

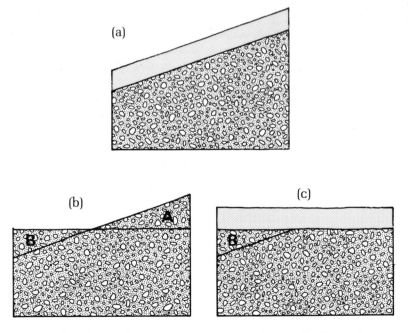

Figure 3: levelling a sloping site – (a) remove all topsoil; (b) transfer subsoil from A to B; (c) replace topsoil

easiest way to tackle the levelling operation is to start by digging out the topsoil at the lowest part of the ground. Place this topsoil in a heap at one side. Then work your way up the slope, removing the topsoil and adding it to the heap; shifting the soil downhill in this way takes the least effort. Now, starting at the highest point, dig out the subsoil, taking it down to the lowest part and placing it on the subsoil which was exposed when you began removing the topsoil. Continue down the slope in this way, taking subsoil from above and using it to build up the lower ground, until the area is level. Finish by spreading the topsoil evenly over the surface, rake it, make any necessary adjustments by scooping out bumps and filling in hollows and rake again to make a firm and even surface (see figure 3). The levelled ground will now be ready to play its part in the new garden design.

A SLOPING SITE

While a gently sloping site may not be too difficult to live with, a steeply sloping one can demand a great deal more effort and become more and more hazardous as time goes by. With age, the uphill climb may become increasingly arduous, especially if there are such things as a wheelbarrow to be pushed, and the downhill incline may become really dangerous for people who are not as steady as they used to be.

An effective and attractive solution to the problem of a sloping site is to divide it into separate areas at different levels. Splitting the garden into "rooms", so that it does not reveal all its attractions at once, is in any case a well established principle of garden design and the effect is often heightened if those rooms are on different levels. There is also the practical consideration that the lawn, which forms a major feature of most gardens, almost demands to be on the level if mowing and general upkeep are to be as easy and effort-free as possible.

The fact must be faced that transforming a sloping site into level sections calls for a great deal of hard work and, the steeper the slope, the greater the labour involved. Although you can do it yourself (see p. 20), there is much to be said for getting the job done by a local contractor with suitable earth-moving equipment; the financial cost may be considerably less than the cost of over-straining oneself.

Steps

To make them as safe as possible and give the user a feeling of confidence, steps should be absolutely firm and fixed; the

23

Steps should be wide with shallow risers and deep treads

slightest wobbliness can lead to disaster. Popular materials for construction are stone slabs and bricks, which should be laid on well prepared foundations (see p. 16 and figure 4). Steps, like paths, should be wide enough to take two people walking side by side and must on no account be too steep. Risers should never be more than 6 in. (15 cm) high and treads should never be less than 13 in. (33 cm) from back to front. It is often recommended that each step should slope slightly downwards from front to back, to give greater stability and reduce wear. Stout handrails at the sides of the steps are a useful precaution against mishaps and, even though you may feel no need of them yet, they could be of assistance in the future for getting up and down.

Ramps

A ramp instead of steps may have advantages for the less mobile and is particularly valuable in providing access for wheeled vehicles, whether wheelchairs or garden barrows. It should have a raised curb on each side to stop wheels running over the edge. There is, however, one snag: a steep ramp is considerably more hazardous and difficult to negotiate than steps. The maximum recommended gradient for safety is 1:12, although 1:20 is a more comfortable slope. This would mean a ramp no less than 20 ft (6 m) long for a difference in level of just 1 ft (30 cm). By com-

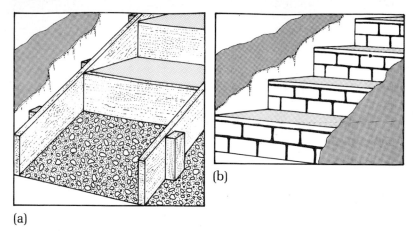

(a)

(b)

Figure 4: constructing steps – (a) concrete; (b) brick and concrete slab

parison, steps would occupy about a tenth of that length, since only two steps would be required to cover the same change of level.

It may sometimes be possible to get from one level to another without either steps or ramps, by having along the side of the site a continuous, gently sloping path, from which cross-walks lead to the different levels and the sections that occupy them. Beside the path, running between it and the fence or other boundary, room could be left for a flower border.

A gently sloping ramp is ideal for less mobile people – a corner of the model garden for the disabled, at the RHS Garden, Wisley

Banks and beds

Some form of embankment will also be needed between different levels. The simplest is a sloping bed and this can be a thoroughly satisfactory solution, enabling the gardener to work from below when tending the plants and so reduce the amount of bending required. Bending can be still further reduced if the lower part of the bed is banked up by stonework or a low wall, perhaps with flat stones on top for sitting on. Be careful not to make the bed (or any other bed in the garden) too wide; you should be able to reach across it comfortably without undue effort.

On a steep bank, where an ordinary flower bed or grass would be impossible to look after, the answer might be to plant prostrate ground-covering shrubs, for instance, juniper, cotoneaster or, if the soil allows, heathers. Vigorous climbers, like ivy and certain honeysuckles, can also be used in these awkward situations.

RETAINING WALLS

Another solution to a sloping site, which involves more time, effort and expense at the construction stage but requires little or no maintenance afterwards, is to build a retaining wall. This is particularly appropriate where the difference in levels is so great that a slope between them would be too steep. The most maintenance-free type of wall is one constructed by setting stones in cement mortar, which prevents them from shifting and stops weeds growing between them. Besides looking somewhat grim, however, this method would rob you of the chance to grow some of the delightful plants that thrive on walls and look their best sprouting from crevices and cascading over the stones.

The construction of a retaining wall without mortar, so that plants can be grown on it, is known as dry walling and is quite simple. The most important thing to remember is that a very considerable weight of earth will be held in place behind the wall, particularly after heavy rain. For this reason, the wall must never be vertical, or the pressure against it may cause it to collapse and topple forwards. It must therefore be built with a decided backward slope from the base to the top.

Begin by digging out a trench 9 in. (23 cm) deep and rather wider than the blocks of stone to be used for building the wall. Half fill this trench with stones, broken brick or any other rubble available, making it slightly higher at the front in order to start the wall with a tilt backwards, and ram it down thoroughly. Place the first layer of stones on this foundation, ensuring that each one rests firmly without wobbling. Cover this layer with 1 in. (2.5 cm) or so of soil and add another course of stones, arranging them so

Left: a retaining wall with rock roses and thyme cascading over the edge
Right: an established rock garden is a delight to the eye and demands little upkeep

that the joints between them do not come directly above the joints between the stones in the layer below. This will strengthen the wall and also improve its appearance. Continue to lay courses of stone in the same way until the wall reaches the height of the ground behind it. For the final layer, it is best to use stones which are somewhat wider than the others from back to front; these will throw heavy rain well back into the earth, instead of allowing it to run down just behind the wall, where it might wash away the soil and weaken the whole structure.

The plants should, if possible, be incorporated into the wall while it is being built. After a course of stones has been laid, complete with its covering of soil, remove the plants from their containers, taking care not to damage the roots, and lay them, with their tops protruding and their roots in the soil, in the joints between adjacent stones, where they will not be crushed when the next stones are lowered into position.

There is a very wide choice of plants that will thrive in a dry wall, including such firm favourites as alyssum, arabis, armeria, aubrieta, campanula, dianthus, iberis, phlox, saxifrage, sedum and sempervivum. Most of these should be available at your local garden centre, where you can see them growing and take your pick. The catalogues issued by alpine nurseries also offer a tempting variety, usual and unusual.

A ROCK GARDEN

A more gradual slope from one level to another makes a perfect site for a rock garden, which not only provides an attractive feature, but is easy to maintain if properly planned and constructed. It can be a boon to those who prefer to enjoy their plants and attend to their needs without having to bend and stretch to do so. An open aspect, facing south or east, is best.

The choice of rock is determined by several factors. If you live near a quarry, it will probably pay you to use the local stone, which can be transported relatively cheaply and is likely to harmonize with its surroundings. Most people, however, will have to buy rock that has been brought from a distance, which can add substantially to the expense; indeed, the transport can cost more than the stone itself. Two generally available types of rock, which may be found at some garden centres, are sandstone and limestone. They are pleasing to look at and have long-lasting qualities. Expense can be kept within bounds and the appearance enhanced by limiting the amount of stone; the old-fashioned rockery used an extravagant amount of material to achieve a highly artificial and forbidding effect, like a giant pudding bristling with jagged stones.

All that is necessary is enough stone to give the appearance of a few outcrops left there by nature rather than by human hand. Starting at the lowest level, place one of the largest pieces of rock as a keystone and tilt it slightly backwards, to heighten the natural impression and encourage rainwater to run back into the soil. From that corner continue to place further stones in alignment with the front edge of the first one, giving each a backward tilt at the same angle. The aim is to make them look as if they all belong to the same underlying rock formation. At the corner where the line was started another line of stones can be laid at right angles, aligned with the side face of the first piece of rock and again given the same slight backward tilt. Each end of the line should bend into the slope and disappear into the soil.

Another tier of rocks can be laid a little further up the slope and then perhaps a third, to give a stepped effect. Do not space these additional layers too far apart; it should be possible, particularly for those whose eyesight is not what it was, to admire and tend the plants at close range, without having to crane or stretch. Be careful to position the stones parallel to those in the first tier, so as to appear to be part of the same natural strata (see figure 5).

Since most alpine plants resent constantly wet conditions at their roots, the soil in the rock garden should be free-draining. If the earth is heavy and inclined to remain wet after rain, lighten it by mixing in plenty of grit or coarse sand. The plants should be set in place in niches between the rocks, as construction proceeds.

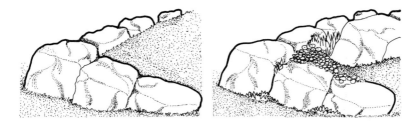

Figure 5: making a rock garden

The variety of plants to choose from is almost unlimited, ranging from small shrubs and dwarf conifers to ground-hugging plants that creep and cascade over the rocks, and from bright-flowered rock roses (*Helianthemum*) to cushion- and rosette-forming plants, such as the multitude of different saxifrages and succulent houseleeks (*Sempervivum*). Once again, it is a good idea to visit your local garden centre or a specialist nursery, where you can see the plants growing and make your choice on the spot.

RAISED BEDS

As we have seen on previous pages, advantage can be taken of natural differences in ground level to create features such as terraces, retaining walls or rock gardens, which can be maintained and enjoyed without bending and stooping. Where the site is flat, then the simplest – indeed perhaps the only – way to provide for those gardeners who cannot or should not stoop is to construct raised beds. These can be built of several different materials, including (in order, from greatest to least attractiveness and unfortunately from highest to lowest cost) natural stone, brick, artificial stone, precast walling blocks and old motor tyres.

Design and construction

Whatever material is used, it is important that the raised bed should not be too wide. A comfortable reach for a person of normal size, without having to stretch unduly, is about 2 ft (60 cm). Therefore, a bed designed to be accessible from either side should be not more than 4 ft (120 cm) across, which will enable the gardener to reach as far as the middle without strain.

So long as this width is not exceeded, a raised bed can be of any length. There are, however, two drawbacks to a long bed, one aesthetic and one practical. The aesthetic objection is that a bed which is over-long in proportion to its width looks monotonous. The practical disadvantage is that having to keep going all the way round from one side to the other of a long bed can be very tiring. The answer is to construct beds whose length is no more than three or four times their width and to arrange them in attractive patterns. Depending on personal preferences and the space available, many different arrangements are possible, from formal geometrical patterns such as two oblong beds in the shape of a T, an L or a V, or three or four beds forming an E (with or without the middle branch), to less formal shapes like a C or an S.

A critical factor in the construction of a raised bed is height. Will the bed be tended or, for that matter, simply enjoyed from a seated position? (This applies not only to those confined to a wheelchair, but also to the large number of people who have some difficulty in walking or who cannot stand for long without feeling tired or dizzy.) If that is the case, then the height of the bed should not exceed 2 ft (60 cm). Any higher would mean that, from a sitting position, the arms would be constantly raised – a sure way to make them ache. If, on the other hand, the bed is to be tended from a standing position, it will need to be higher, in order to avoid the discomfort and possible harm caused by having to stoop. In that instance, the height of the bed can be raised to 3 ft (90 cm).

There is much to be said for topping the walls of a raised bed, particularly one built of stone, with slabs which are wide enough (and stable enough) to sit on while attending to the plants. However, it is vital that the wall should be sufficiently low for the sitter's feet to be planted firmly on the ground. Dangling one's feet in the air can all too easily lead to toppling backwards, risking at least damage to the plants and at worst injury to the owner of the

Opposite above: raised beds can be arranged in various shapes
Below: a raised bed is a perfect home for alpines and a layer of coarse grit on the surface helps to reduce evaporation

feet. To enable a person of normal height to sit on the wall with his or her feet on the ground, the wall should be no higher than 2½ ft (75 cm).

The site for a raised bed will be dictated largely by the size and shape of the garden. Preferably, it should be in an open position. Although a little light shade during part of the day may be acceptable to many plants, heavy shadow from buildings or overhanging trees, with consequent drip during rainy weather, is to be avoided.

To make it as easy and pleasant as possible to look after, whether from a seated or a standing position, the raised bed should be flanked by paving or a hard surface, laid right up against the wall and preferably at least 4 ft (120 cm) wide. The area where the actual bed is to come is left unpaved, to allow for unimpeded drainage.

The method of construction depends on the material used. Dry walling with natural stone produces the most attractive results and is based on the same principles as when building a retaining wall (see p. 26). Once again, the stones should be laid with a decided slope into the bed. Walls of brick, artificial stone or precast walling blocks should be built vertically, with a concrete foundation on a base of well rammed hardcore (see p. 16). The bricks or blocks will need to be laid in mortar, consisting of one part of cement to five or six parts of builder's sand, mixed with enough water to form a smooth paste; the addition of a little plasticizer will make it buttery and easier to spread. As work progresses, be sure to check with a spirit-level that each course is level.

It is a wise precaution to give a long bed added strength, by means of buttresses inside the bed. These are securely bonded into the side walls at intervals of 4 or 5 ft (120–150 cm) and will not be visible once the bed is completely filled with soil.

Old motor tyres may sound unpromising material for a raised bed, but they can be made to look quite pleasant if given a good coat or two of weatherproof paint; white or stone-colour are perhaps the most suitable. As well as being cheap, tyres have the advantage of being quick and easy to erect and dismantle and they can be useful as holders for plants, both upright and trailing, in such situations as flanking a garden seat. The tyres are built up in different sizes, with the largest, naturally, at the bottom. The average car tyre has an overall diameter of about 22 in. (56 cm), which gives a bed some 16 in. (40 cm) across between the inner rims. Old lorry tyres will provide more planting space still.

Soil and plants

The type of soil to be used in a raised bed will depend on what plants are to be grown in it. For the general run of popular garden plants – perennials, bedding plants, bulbs and perhaps some vegetables and soft fruit – ordinary, good, loamy topsoil will be quite suitable. It would, however, be a pity to miss the opportunity of filling the bed with something rather better than average garden soil, which can usually do with some improvement. The ideal mixture would resemble the well tried and trusted John Innes potting compost No. 3, which consists of seven parts by volume of sterilized loam, three parts of moss peat and two parts of sand, plus fertilizer and chalk. This can be bought ready made from garden suppliers, but to fill a sizable bed with it would be horrifyingly expensive. A cheaper, but quite satisfactory, alternative is to use ordinary garden soil mixed with peat and sand in roughly the above proportions. If the soil is heavy, increase the amount of sand; if light, increase the amount of peat.

Though a soil mixture of this kind will do very well for a large number of plants, modifications may need to be made for special purposes. A raised bed is ideal for growing a collection of alpines and since these prefer a more rapidly draining medium, some coarse grit should be added to the mixture. (For further details of the cultivation of alpines in raised beds, see the Wisley handbook, *Alpines the easy way.*) Alternatively, if the bed is to be used for lime-hating plants, such as azaleas and most heathers, then it is essential to give them a lime-free soil mixture. Remember, too, that it is best to water these plants with rainwater; hard tapwater can be very harmful to them.

Part of the Help the Aged Garden at the Chelsea Show, 1987

Container gardening

For those with a limited amount of strength, energy, time or space – or, for that matter, those who have plentiful supplies of all four, but who like to explore different ways of growing plants and displaying them to best advantage – there are many types of container available. Container gardening is gardening reduced to manageable proportions. Although it may demand quite a lot of initial preparation and subsequent maintenance, it does not involve strenuous digging, large-scale weeding or other laborious tasks. Containers, like raised beds, bring the soil to a more convenient height, at which plants can be cultivated and appreciated more easily. They can be placed in the most accessible position for the gardener, by a path, for example, or on a patio near the house, where they are close at hand and visible from indoors. They can even be moved around on a trolley.

TROUGHS AND SINKS

The stone troughs used as drinking and feeding receptacles for animals in days gone by make ideal containers, particularly for growing alpines and rock plants. Such troughs could once be had for next to nothing, but the few that can still be found now fetch astronomical prices.

Old-fashioned glazed sinks are less expensive substitutes, though even they are no longer cheap unless you are lucky enough to find one going begging in a builder's yard. Sinks have one advantage over troughs: they already have a plughole to provide the necessary drainage, whereas troughs, made for the sole purpose of retaining water, must have drainage holes added. These should be driven through the bottom with a cold chisel or a large masonry drill – an arduous task which requires great care, to avoid fracturing the stone.

Disguising a glazed sink

An untreated glazed sink is a very unappealing sight, but covering it with a mixture known as hypertufa can transform its appearance to that of mellow weathered stone. The method is quite simple. First wash the sink very thoroughly, being particularly careful to remove any grease which might prevent the covering from adhering properly; a little washing-up liquid will help, so long as it is well rinsed off afterwards. Leave the sink until it is thoroughly dry. Then paint the outside and 3 or 4 in. (7.5–10 cm) down the inside with a suitable bonding material; the proprietary adhesive Unibond is excellent for the purpose. When the adhesive is almost dry but still tacky to touch, plaster the treated surface with a good coating, about ½ in. (1 cm) thick, of a paste consisting of equal parts of sharp sand, moss peat and cement mixed thoroughly together with enough water to make a fairly stiff dough. Do not attempt to make the coating too smooth, since a rough surface will give a more natural appearance.

If the hypertufa dries out too quickly, it will go the colour of concrete. Stand the treated sink in a cool shady place and let it take a week or two to dry, so that the hypertufa develops a warm friendly colour. As time goes by, the hypertufa should provide just the right environment for the growth of mosses and lichens, which will disguise its artificial nature and give it an attractively weathered look. To encourage and speed up the process, a film of milk, or of water in which rice has been boiled, can be brushed or sprayed over the surface and left to dry.

As interest in the growing of plants in troughs has been greatly increasing in recent years, some firms are manufacturing modern versions in various materials, from natural or artificial stone to fibreglass and plastic. Many garden centres offer a selection and there is usually a range on display at major horticultural shows. As always, the most attractive and durable are likely to be the most expensive and the cheapest are almost certain to be the ugliest and flimsiest.

Siting and support

A trough or sink must be put in position before being filled with soil. It will be quite heavy enough even when empty and, when it is full, you could do yourself an injury if you try to move it. The site it is to occupy should be chosen both to show it off to advantage, so that it commands attention, and to be easy to get at when you want to look after, or simply look at, the plants. It should stand on a paved area or hard surface – for instance, beside a path, next to some steps or on a terrace or patio. A trough can also make an attractive feature on a lawn, in which case it should be surrounded by paving sunk just below the level of the grass in order not to impede mowing.

The trough should be mounted on some kind of plinth or pillars, which will prevent the drainage holes becoming blocked and give it greater "presence". It is most important that the support is

35

Above (left): a trough or sink offers a delightful form of gardening in miniature; (right) a sink garden mounted on supports and surrounded by paving
Below: even old car tyres can be converted into containers and built up to a convenient height

strong and firm enough to bear the combined weight of the trough and the soil inside it. Concrete or walling blocks can be used, but it is generally found that brick or stone are the most satisfactory, for appearance as well as strength. Whatever material is chosen, the trough must be placed squarely on it so that it cannot move. It should project 4 or 5 in. (10–12 cm) beyond the plinth on each side; this will help to conceal the support and allow one to get nearer the trough when tending the plants.

A great advantage of a trough or sink is that it can be raised to the right height for plants to be inspected at close quarters and attended to in comfort. However, one has to consider the height of the plinth in relation to the depth of the trough, otherwise the whole structure might appear unbalanced and top-heavy. An old sink 10 in. (25 cm) deep overall (quite a common measurement) looks best if the top edge is about 18 in. (45 cm) above the ground, which means that the plinth can be no more than 8 in. (20 cm) high. This is a reasonable height for someone working from a seat or wheelchair, if they do not mind stretching a bit.

For those people who are not as supple as they were and have difficulty stooping or kneeling, the trough would need to be higher (and correspondingly larger, ideally, for a balanced effect). A height of 2 to 2½ ft (60–75 cm) above the ground should enable them to operate easily when standing upright. If the plinth itself is some 20 in. (50 cm) high, it would be possible for a chair to be placed directly in front of the trough, as at a table, with sufficient clearance for the person's legs underneath. This could help to overcome the problem of gardening from a sitting position, which normally involves twisting round or stretching awkwardly to reach the plants, even though the sink (or raised bed) might be at a convenient height.

Soil and plants

When the plinth has been built and the trough set in place on top of it, the next thing to do before putting in the soil is to cover the drainage holes with some good-sized pieces of broken pot, hollow side downwards; this is to allow water to drain away without carrying the soil with it.

Alpines are supremely well suited to growing in a trough or sink. It is of great importance that the soil mixture should drain freely, since nothing is worse for them than prolonged wetness at the roots. An excellent mixture for most of the popular alpines is composed of four parts of John Innes potting compost No. 2 (obtainable from most garden suppliers) and one part of coarse grit, mixed together thoroughly. A 2 in. (5 cm) layer of gravel should first be spread over the bottom, followed by a light covering of rough peat or leaf mould. Over this spread a layer of the soil mixture, firm it down very thoroughly, add another layer, firm that down, and so on until the trough is filled to just below the top edge. You can create a miniature landscape by inserting into the soil a few pieces of rock, which will also provide for certain plants the cool moist root-run they prefer.

There is a very wide range of plants suitable for sinks and troughs and it is a good plan to visit garden centres and nurseries, where you can see the plants in flower and choose the ones you fancy. Pay several visits at intervals during the year, so that you can select something for each season and avoid having all the plants at their best simultaneously. (For further details of growing alpines in sinks and troughs, see the Wisley handbook, *Alpines the easy way*.)

OTHER TYPES OF CONTAINER

Window boxes, urns, tubs, hanging baskets and other ornamental containers give opportunities for everyone, no matter how restricted in space or mobility, to grow and enjoy plants. There are many different kinds of container, old and new, designed specifically for growing plants and made in every conceivable material – stone and marble (mostly simulated these days, not always with marked success), terracotta, metal, wood and plastic. There are also containers used originally for quite different purposes, such as discarded tyres (see p. 32), barrels, old chimney pots and earthenware drainpipes.

Garden centres and an increasing number of department stores have on sale a selection of containers, most produced in quantity and priced to give the retailer a satisfactory profit. It may be better to do a bit of bargain hunting in junk yards and second-hand shops and at sales. You might even find something suitable among your own possessions. That old brass coal-scuttle, for instance, made redundant by the central heating, could be the perfect foil for a brilliant geranium, or its glint could liven up a fern or two.

Container gardening can take up a fair amount of time and energy. Annuals and bedding plants, which are the most popular choice, must be bought in or raised from seed, hardened off if necessary, planted in the container and then watered, fed and deadheaded regularly. In hot weather, containers dry out very quickly and hanging baskets, in particular, may need watering twice a day. An alternative to spring-flowering bulbs and annuals, which last only a short time and have to be replaced, is to use longer-term plants for a permanent display, which requires less

Containers can be used almost anywhere to bring a touch of colour

maintenance. These could include perennials like hostas, for foliage effect as well as flowers, bold evergreen shrubs such as *Fatsia japonica*, dwarf conifers for winter interest and even a clematis to climb up a trellis.

Containers offer scope for imaginative planting. Tender plants, for example, which might otherwise be unpractical to grow, can be enjoyed and then moved indoors for the winter; and lime-hating plants like camellias, which would not succeed in a garden with chalky soil, can be given suitable compost. Containers are an excellent way to brighten up a dull spot or add variety to a flat expanse of paving. Finally, with so many shapes and sizes available, it should be possible to get a container of the right height for comfortable gardening, whether it is a window box or an urn on a pedestal. (For further information, see the Wisley handbook, *Gardening in ornamental containers*.)

Gardening under cover

GREENHOUSES

As you get older and the weather seems to get steadily worse, compared with your memories of what it was like when you were young, the idea of gardening under cover, where you and your plants can enjoy a better climate than the one outside, becomes very attractive.

Before spending any of your savings on a greenhouse, however, it is just as well to consider whether you will gain the hoped-for benefits from your investment. Though a greenhouse can bring a great deal of extra pleasure, it will bring extra work as well. It will tie you down too, because it needs constant attention, even when equipped with the latest devices that are claimed by the makers to enable the greenhouse to run itself. So, before buying one, ask yourself: (a) whether you are prepared to give it the extra time and effort it demands; and (b) whether there is a kind neighbour or a friend living near who can be trusted to look after it when you are away – otherwise, you will have to give up holidays.

The hard fact is that plants growing in the ground outside will usually thrive, or at least survive, with little or no attention (and if they do not thrive, you can always blame the weather), whereas in a greenhouse they are forced to rely on you. Also, a greenhouse can provide a perfect breeding ground for pests and diseases, where they multiply in ideal conditions at a horrifying rate.

Basic requirements

If, in spite of these discouragements, you still want a greenhouse, there are some practical considerations to be borne in mind in the choice of position, type and materials. Whatever kind is selected, it should be sited away from the shadow of trees and buildings, yet close enough to the house so that you do not have to struggle far, in all weathers, to get to it.

Greenhouses are of two basic kinds – free-standing and lean-to. Of the free-standing type, the most popular are those with a span roof, which are usually sold in sections to be put together by the buyer. Many can be easily extended if your enthusiasm for greenhouse gardening should grow. Hexagonal or octagonal models are becoming increasingly popular and are often handsome enough to be incorporated into the garden design as features in their own right. Although they offer less growing space, they could be the answer in a small garden.

Lean-to greenhouses, consisting of three sides and a single-span roof, are built against a wall, which forms the fourth side. They are usually recommended for a south-facing wall, but can face any direction if suitable plants are grown.

The traditional greenhouse structure has long been of wood, now mainly western red cedar, which is highly resistant to rot and only needs treating with preservative every five years or so to keep it looking smart. For a trouble-free if less attractive greenhouse, however, there is nothing to beat aluminium, which requires almost no maintenance and is practically indestructible (although it may corrode in seaside areas).

In choosing a greenhouse that will continue to satisfy your requirements, while allowing for possible changes in your needs as the years go by, a very important factor is the entrance. There should be no step or other obstacle to trip you up or impede your progress as you go in and out. Unfortunately, many greenhouses, especially metal ones, have a sill across the entrance and the only way to get round this would be to build a ramp. It is sound sense, too, for the doorway to be wide enough for a wheelchair or walking frame to pass through without difficulty, even if you require neither of these aids at the moment. As for the greenhouse door, there are three good reasons for choosing a sliding rather than a hinged one. First, opening and closing a sliding door requires practically no effort and can be done with the tip of a finger. Secondly, it cannot bang to and fro, risking broken glass. Thirdly, it takes up no space, whether open or closed.

The path, both leading to the greenhouse and inside it, should be firm, even and level, preferably made of concrete or paving slabs. It is often advised that the floor should be of something rough and able to soak up water, such as clinker or bare earth, which can be sprayed in the summer to increase humidity; but this is apt to become slippery and it is better to be safe than sorry.

The height and width of the greenhouse bench should be decided by what is most comfortable and causes the least strain. If you are going to be seated, the standard bench is likely to be too high and would be better lowered, so that you do not have to raise your arms. Similarly, you may find it best to have a narrower bench than usual in order to reach plants at the back. If, on the other hand, you will be standing when working, make sure that there is enough head room and you won't have to stoop.

For permanence combined with economy, there is at present nothing to rival glass as a greenhouse covering. Flexible plastic sheeting is initially cheaper, but it quickly deteriorates and needs replacing, involving you in additional expense not only of money but of time and effort. One recently developed glazing material, which is being used increasingly instead of glass, despite its higher cost, is twin-wall polycarbonate sheeting. This is almost as transparent as glass, but much lighter and stronger, provides excellent insulation against heat loss and can be easily cut to size with a knife or hacksaw.

Heating

When considering the question of heating, you must first decide what temperature you wish to maintain. Is your greenhouse going to be unheated, frost-free, cold, cool, intermediate or warm? To set against the additional expense (which rises with the temperature) is the fact that heating extends the range of plants that can be grown and also makes the greenhouse a pleasanter place to be in during winter.

A greenhouse with no artificial heating at all will not be frost-free and can only accommodate plants that are not damaged by temperatures below freezing point. It is therefore ideal for alpines, the reason for growing them under glass being not to protect them from the cold, which they relish, but to shield them from the wet, which can be fatal to them. Some retired people have found a new and absorbing interest in cultivating these fascinating plants – an interest made more enjoyable by not having to worry about heating bills. (For details of alpine houses and what can be grown in them, see the Wisley handbook, *Alpines the easy way*.)

By giving the greenhouse just enough heat to keep it frost-free, you can use it during the winter to house early-flowering chrysanthemums or fuchsias; to overwinter near-hardy bedding plants such as antirrhinums, sown in late summer, for an earlier display than a spring sowing can give; to produce an early crop of lettuce or carrots; or even to maintain a cactus collection.

The cool greenhouse, with a minimum temperature of 45°F (7°C) throughout the winter, is perhaps the most worthwhile for the ordinary gardener and has many uses. It is suitable for some of the popular winter-flowering pot plants, like cinerarias and cyclamen, and for perpetual-flowering carnations. It can also be used for overwintering half-hardy perennials such as geraniums

Opposite above: a greenhouse with a sliding door and without a sill, standing on a hard surface
Below: an unheated greenhouse filled with a range of alpines and choice plants

(pelargoniums) and for producing super-early lettuces when the shop ones are at their most expensive.

The intermediate greenhouse, with a minimum temperature of between 50° and 55°F (10–13°C), enables you to grow a wider range of plants, including exotic foliage plants and orchids, while the warm greenhouse, with a minimum of between 55° and 60°F (13–15°C) or more, broadens the scope still further to embrace tropical and sub-tropical plants.

Personal taste is only one factor in deciding what plants to grow. Another is how much it would cost to grow them. The harsh reality is that, each time you raise the minimum temperature a mere 5 degrees F (2.5 degrees C), you double your heating bill. In other words, a warm greenhouse will cost you between eight and sixteen times as much to heat as one that is kept just frost-free.

Faced with today's high fuel costs, many people on a limited income heat their greenhouses only in spring, from the beginning of March to May, just enough to stop the temperature falling below 45°F (7°C). This enables them to start tubers of such pot plants as begonias and gloxinias into growth and to make early sowings of some of the hardy and near-hardy annuals, plus leeks and onions, for planting out later. Half-hardy annuals will need more heat; but to save the expense of heating the whole greenhouse by those costly extra degrees, the seeds can be sown in a small, electrically heated propagator, which uses very little current. More economical still, they can be germinated on a windowsill in a warm room indoors, sowing them in a pot or tray of seed compost and then covering with a sheet of glass or enclosing in a polythene bag to prevent drying out. Once they have germinated, which is what requires the extra heat, the seedlings can be pricked out and grown on in the cool greenhouse until time to plant out. However, you should perhaps ask yourself whether it is worth raising your own bedding plants, when you can buy them quite cheaply at planting time, without the bother of housing and looking after them until then.

Different methods of heating all have their advocates, but there are three very strong arguments in favour of electricity – convenience, cultural conditions and cost. For convenience, electricity is unrivalled: you have no fuel to carry or wicks to trim and thermostatic control enables you to set the required temperature so that the heater switches itself on and off automatically and keeps energy consumption to a minimum. Cultural conditions in an electrically heated greenhouse are favourable both for plant growth and for anyone tending the plants; there are none of the fumes and excessive humidity that so often accompany gas or paraffin heaters. Electric fan-heaters are especially good, as they circulate the air and reduce the risk of plant disease caused by a stagnant atmosphere.

The cost of heating a greenhouse by electricity compares very favourably with that of heating by other means, particularly if you choose the Economy 7 system, based on a substantially lower unit price at night than during the day. Electric heaters can be considerably cheaper to run than paraffin or bottled gas heaters, largely because the latter must have ample ventilation, in order to get rid of fumes and excess humidity and to supply sufficient air to operate. Unfortunately, all this ventilation lets out not only the fumes but a great deal of the expensively produced heat.

Electricity always should be installed by a qualified electrician, which is a further expense. To add to its advantages, however, is the fact that electricity makes it possible to use many other devices which are designed to help you get the most out of your greenhouse, such as a small propagator, soil-warming cables (themselves a very economical form of heating), a mist propagation unit and, of course, lighting. If, on the other hand, the deciding factor has to be the initial cost of the equipment or its installation, then a paraffin heater, with all its drawbacks, is probably the least expensive alternative.

As a general rule, it is much cheaper to heat a lean-to greenhouse than a free-standing one of the same capacity. Not only is far less heat lost through the back wall than through the glass but, if the lean-to faces south, the wall will absorb heat on sunny days and give it out at night, thus reducing the amount of artificial heat needed. The installation of a heating system in a lean-to attached to your house should also be easier and less expensive, particularly if it can be an extension to an existing central heating system.

Management

There are many other tasks involved in managing a greenhouse successfully. Good ventilation is essential at all times of year and should be adjusted according to the weather. Shading may have to be applied to the glass in late spring to keep the temperature down and humidity will need to be increased in the summer. Above all, plants must be watered. In some cases, there are short cuts to help save time and labour at relatively little cost. Ventilation, for example, can be controlled by a simple device which is activated by temperature changes to open and close the windows. Watering can be automated by an elaborate and expensive system or, just as efficiently and much more cheaply, by standing the plant pots on

45

capillary matting – an absorbent material which draws up water from a reservoir. (For further information about greenhouses generally, see the Wisley handbook, *The small greenhouse*.)

HOME EXTENSIONS AND CONSERVATORIES

A lean-to that is accessible only through its own external door has the same disadvantage as a free-standing greenhouse: to reach it you have first to go outside, however unpleasant the weather may be. It is well worth considering whether to make a door through to the lean-to from the house, so that you never have to get wet or cold in going from one to the other and the plants are not subjected to chilling blasts as you do so.

When a lean-to is integrated into the house in this way it tends to be called something else – a home extension, a sun room or, on a somewhat grander scale, a conservatory. The most satisfactory are usually those designed as part of the house (which, with such a desirable built-in feature, is likely to be up-market, both in style and price). For those who wish to add an extension to a house at present without one, there is a very wide range of models available, mostly sold in prefabricated sections for home assembly and often advertised in gardening magazines. It is obviously best to choose a wall of the house which already has a doorway, ideally one with glazed single or double doors leading on to a terrace, which can serve as a ready-laid floor to the extension when it is in place. If a new doorway has to be made through the wall, the work should be done by an experienced and reliable builder. It is also important, when undertaking any substantial structural alterations or additions to your property, to obtain the necessary planning permission from the local authority.

The pleasure that an extension to the house can give goes far beyond enjoyment of the plants grown in it, especially for those people who would be unwise, unable or unwilling to venture out in harsh weather. To sit at your ease in the extension, conservatory or whatever you care to call it, with the sun shining in through the glass and a little supplementary warmth from the heating system, can make a cold winter's day seem like a warm spring one.

Opposite above: a lean-to which can be reached from the house has many advantages
Below: a conservatory can be enjoyed throughout the year and whatever the weather

HOUSEPLANTS

The growing of houseplants is still by far the most popular form of indoor gardening. Recent surveys show that about eight households in every ten have plants in the home. The reason is, of course, that houseplants can be grown and enjoyed by all, whether they live in a house, a flat or one room and whether they have a garden or not.

Elderly people often find great pleasure in having plants around them, enjoying not only their appearance but the feeling of companionship their presence can give and the sense of achievement that comes from tending them and watching them thrive as a result. An added source of satisfaction, particularly to those on a limited income, is that heating costs for houseplants are practically nil, since the plants share the warmth already provided in the home for the human occupants. The minimum temperature at which a room needs to be maintained for comfort is equivalent to that of a warm greenhouse and consequently many tropical plants can now be grown in even the most modest home, as long as the atmosphere is not too dry.

This form of gardening has obvious attractions for those who are confined to the house or whose mobility is limited. It is a year-round activity, unaffected by the weather, and does not demand hard physical work. The indoor gardener requires few tools and can take advantage of lightweight peat-based composts and plastic pots. It is surprising, too, how many humble domestic objects can be transformed into decorative containers for houseplants.

Like other plants grown under cover, houseplants are entirely dependent on you for the provision of light, warmth, water, humidity and food. Some of these basic needs will be met by choosing the right plant for the right place – a flowering plant for a windowsill and a foliage plant for a shady corner, for instance. With a little thought and care it is possible to select a plant to match conditions in almost any part of the house.

Apart from siting plants according to their preference, there are many ways to reduce routine tasks. Humidity can be maintained by growing plants in groups or standing the pots on gravel in a saucer of water. Instead of regular liquid feeding, nutrients can be supplied over a long period by a slow-release fertilizer, available in the form of sticks, tablets or granules. Self-watering containers make watering less of a chore and are particularly useful if you are away on holiday. (For further details of growing houseplants, see the Wisley handbook, *Houseplants*.)

Tools and equipment

TOOLS

The most important requirements when choosing tools are that they should be strong and easy to use and particularly so if the owner is getting on in years. Cheap tools are apt to have a short life and can be dangerous; a blade or handle that suddenly snaps may throw an elderly person off balance, giving at least a fright and at worst a severe injury.

The best tools are all too often the most expensive, in the initial outlay at least, but they may well be the most economical in the end because they are likely to last much longer. So it is better to spend your money on a few really good tools rather than on a lot of inferior ones. If you cannot afford them yourself, let it be known that they would be excellent presents.

Probably the greatest single contribution in recent years to making gardening less arduous has been the introduction of stainless steel tools. A stainless steel spade goes into the ground cleanly without sticking, stays sharp and is so much easier to use than the old-fashioned kind that, in spite of its higher cost, many people, especially those whose strength and energy are not what they were, would consider it indispensable. The same may be said of forks and most of the other usual garden tools: choose stainless steel ones if you possibly can.

Another major improvement is the use of lightweight, yet extremely strong, alloys and similar materials for shafts and handles, which has resulted in modern tools being less heavy and cumbersome than their predecessors. Since needs and preferences vary, it is important to select tools that suit you. Insist on handling them before you buy and compare as many makes as possible for size, lightness, balance and general feel, until you find one with which you are entirely comfortable.

In addition to the usual garden implements for able-bodied people, there are now a great many tools specially designed to make gardening possible, and indeed pleasurable, for those whose physical disabilities would otherwise curtail their activities. They include long-handled spades, forks, shears, trowels and hand forks, which can be used from a standing position without bending or from a chair, and a similar range of short-handled tools for such jobs as cultivating raised beds. Some have telescopic handles so that the length can be adjusted. There are

49

also many different devices to make hoeing easier and less tiring.

For people who find it difficult to grip, there are now tools with bulbous, T-shaped and padded handles, which are much easier to grasp than normal ones by hands afflicted with muscular weakness. There are numerous tools intended to give extra purchase to weak hands. A recent development for those who are unable to exert enough force to use ordinary pruners is a pair of secateurs which works by a simple ratchet action, building up pressure through a series of gentle squeezes. Among devices for those who can use only one hand are a handle-grip, which makes one-handed digging possible, a long-handled cutter, which cuts flowers and holds them until the trigger is released, and a weed puller operating on the same principle.

EQUIPMENT

Many other pieces of equipment can make life easier for the not-so-young gardener, whether suffering from any physical disability or not. A special grab like a pair of scissors enables you to pick up a pile of leaves, weeds or grass mowings and dispose of it neatly without having to stoop. There is also a stool with a mat, which has proved a blessing to thousands of gardeners since it first came on the market several years ago. One way up, it serves as a light-weight portable seat, on which you can rest your weight when you feel like it; the other way up, it becomes a low platform for kneeling, with strong arms on both sides to help you lever yourself up again (see figures 6 and 7).

Old-fashioned metal watering cans have been largely replaced by lighter plastic ones. Water, however, is still as heavy as ever and the only way to reduce the amount of water you have to carry is to choose smaller cans which hold less. There are various types of equipment to make watering easier and quicker, ranging from ordinary hose pipes and sprinklers to complete irrigation systems. A useful invention is the perforated hose, which can be laid permanently along the edge of a border. However, in these days of water shortages, the use of hoses and sprinklers is often restricted, just when they are most needed, and it may only be possible to water plants individually with a can. A garden tap is always a good idea.

Traditional wooden wheelbarrows, which often weigh as much as or even more than the loads they carry, are very unwieldy compared with the newer types, which are made of lighter materials and require much less effort. With an ascender barrow, the lifting of heavy loads is a thing of the past: simply by releasing a catch, the container part is lowered to the ground so that

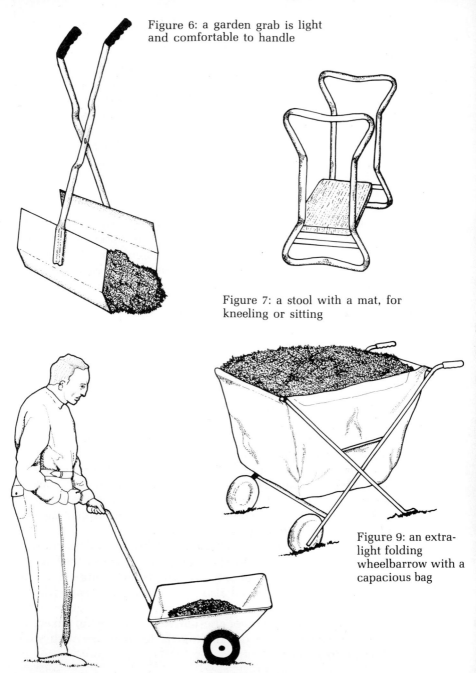

Figure 6: a garden grab is light and comfortable to handle

Figure 7: a stool with a mat, for kneeling or sitting

Figure 9: an extra-light folding wheelbarrow with a capacious bag

Figure 8: a two-wheeled barrow gives stability and has a single long handle so that it can be used without bending

51

rubbish can be swept, raked or shovelled into it; when full, it is lifted into place by pulling back the easy-grip handles. Among other designs that reduce strain are two-wheeled barrows of various sizes. These can be a real boon, not only because of their carrying capacity, but because they provide stability and support for those whose walking is unsteady. There are also ultra-light-weight barrows, consisting of a large, tough, woven bag fixed to a tubular metal frame on wheels. The bag can be detached and used separately or folded away, while on some space-saving models the frame itself can be folded neatly for storing and hung up with the garden tools (see figures 8 and 9, p. 51).

One of the afflictions of advancing years is that we become increasingly subject to lapses of memory and, as a result, tend to leave things about. If this happens outdoors and a tool is left out in bad weather, it may soon deteriorate before its absence is noticed and could cause an accident if it trips someone up. A simple and practical solution is to hang all tools in their places and then paint the outline of each one on the wall behind it. When you come to put the tools away, you can see at a glance whether any are missing.

MACHINERY

The question of garden machinery is a tricky one. Electrically powered machines undoubtedly save time and labour in jobs like lawn mowing and hedge cutting, but all are potentially dangerous and may prove difficult to control in elderly hands. Hover mowers, in particular, can run away with the less agile. Although most electrical appliances must comply with certain standards and usually have built-in safety features, precautions should always be observed. They must never be used when it is raining and great care should be taken to avoid severing the cable. A residual circuit breaker should also be fitted to protect against electric shock if anything does go wrong.

Instead of using possibly hazardous electrical equipment, why not pay local garden maintenance contractors to mow the lawn or cut the hedge? This will not only save you from having to buy and look after the machinery, but also stop your relations and friends worrying about whether you might overtax your strength and run the risk of accidents. Another alternative, if you feel the upkeep of a lawn or hedge is too demanding, is to dispense with such features altogether.

Low-maintenance gardening

DEFEATING WEEDS

The one thing on which gardeners everywhere agree is that the most tiresome and worrying aspect of running a garden is controlling the weeds. For those whose strength and vigour are not what they were it is particularly distressing if, despite all their loving attention to the plants, the garden can no longer be kept free of weeds and tidy.

Cultivation

The traditional method of dealing with weeds is cultivation – in other words, the destruction of weeds by physical means, from uprooting them by hand to the use of hoes and other tools. It can be very effective and even curiously satisfying. It is, however, the most time-consuming and arduous way of tackling weeds and the sort of task that can make retired people feel as if they have given up being wage-earning drudges to become unpaid gardening drudges instead.

Ground cover

Ground cover is a much more satisfactory and pleasant method of control. It is also the most natural. The trouble with many gardens is that a great deal of the ground between cultivated plants is left bare, which is not only a waste of space, but an open invitation to weeds. The most efficient groundcover plants are those which establish dominance of the territory within the first season after planting, so that the weeds cannot compete because they are denied space, light and nourishment. Foremost among these are quick-growing evergreens of dense twiggy habit, such as ivies and selected forms of the lesser periwinkle, *Vinca minor*. It may be necessary to do some weeding round them in the early stages after planting but, once established, they should hardly ever need it again.

Other dense-growing evergreens of somewhat less rapid growth may require weeding for another season or two before they provide complete ground cover; they may also benefit from some initial pruning to encourage branching near the ground. Examples are the popular gold dust, *Alyssum saxatile (Aurinia*

Left: the lesser periwinkle, *Vinca minor*, is a very useful ground cover plant
Right: a mulch of polythene covered with processed bark and peat can be both attractive and effective

saxatilis), dwarf junipers, winter flowering heaths and *Euonymus fortunei* var. *radicans*, whose brightly variegated cultivars will tolerate deep shade.

As well as the large range of evergreen carpeting and hummock-forming plants, there are several deciduous ones which, although leafless in winter, soon develop a thick weed-defying cover during the growing season. A few weed seedlings may appear before the foliage is fully grown, but are easily dealt with if you remove them as soon as you notice them. These useful perennials include hostas, many of the true geraniums or cranesbills and the ever popular lady's mantle, *Alchemilla mollis*, with its rounded softly downy leaves surmounted by sprays of dainty flowers like greenish yellow stars.

The use of groundcover plants has increased greatly in recent years and garden centres are able to offer a good selection suitable for local conditions of soil and climate. (For further advice on cultivation and a list of suitable plants, see the Wisley handbook, *Ground cover plants*.)

Mulching

An alternative to living ground cover is a mulch of organic matter, such as peat, garden compost, leaf mould or processed bark. It is spread over the soil in a layer 2 to 3 in. (5–7.5 cm) thick and suppresses weeds by robbing them of light. In places where appearance does not matter, such as between fruit bushes or in a vegetable plot, covering the ground with a mulch of black polythene sheeting is an easy and highly effective weed deterrent; it is also good round newly planted trees and shrubs.

Chemicals

The most controversial method of weed control is by means of chemicals. Although many people are reluctant to use them, for fear of damage to the environment, there is no doubt that chemical weedkillers can be a blessing, particularly for those gardeners with limited energy and physical endurance.

There are several different herbicides on the market and it is vitally important to choose the right one for the job. However, you can easily make do with one or two in the average garden. For dealing with annual weeds in flower beds, vegetable rows and among shrubs and for cleaning up ground before sowing or planting, the paraquat and diquat mixture is very useful. It destroys all leafy growth with which it comes in contact and must therefore be applied with great care, to avoid spray drifting on to garden plants. It is inactivated once it reaches the soil.

Glyphosate in another herbicide which does not persist in the soil but, unlike paraquat and diquat, it is absorbed by the leaves and taken down to the roots, killing the whole plant. It has proved invaluable in treating those difficult perennial weeds with creeping underground parts. It is also available in a handy gel form, which can be painted on the leaves of weeds growing in awkward places without risk of damage to neighbouring plants.

In addition to these, there are weedkillers designed for specific situations. Lawn care has been revolutionized by the introduction of selective weedkillers, which kill broad-leaved weeds without harming the grass. It is now possible to have a sward to be proud of, with none of the back-breaking effort of grubbing out tough weeds – often spoiling the lawn at the same time. Again, the herbicide must be applied very carefully and must not be allowed to drift on to plants other than grasses. Similarly, special formulations exist for paths, drives and paved areas, which keep them weed-free for a whole season and end the chore of extracting weeds from between slabs.

Like all other powerful chemicals, herbicides must be handled, stored and used with great care. It is a sensible precaution to wear rubber gloves when handling them and to wash your hands very thoroughly after use. Always store them out of harm's way, where children and pets cannot find them. Above all, before starting to use any weedkiller, read the instructions on the container carefully, down to the very last word, and obey them to the letter. Use the correct dose and no more; never be tempted to add a little extra for luck. (For further information, see the Wisley handbook, *Weed control in the garden*.)

DIGGING AND WATERING

Digging and watering are two other tasks which can occupy much of the gardener's time and energy and it is possible to make both more manageable in various ways. On a new site, preparation and improvement of the soil, by incorporating organic matter, are essential, but once you have achieved a permanent planting of shrubs and perennials, digging will be unnecessary. A lot depends on the choice of plants.

Ground cover, of course, dispenses with digging altogether and has the bonus of reducing evaporation from the soil caused by wind and sun, as well as suppressing weeds. Mulching performs the same service (see also p. 53 and p. 54).

WHAT TO GROW

Trees and shrubs

In deciding what to grow in your retirement garden, you face a dilemma, particularly with the trees and shrubs which form the framework of the design. On the one hand, they should grow quickly enough to produce a reasonably finished effect, which you can enjoy without having to wait too long. On the other hand, rapid growers can be much too exuberant and need a great deal of work to keep under control. A compromise is necessary, therefore, between the too fast and too slow.

Before buying a tree or shrub, you should consider not only its rate of growth, but its ultimate height and spread, so that you can space it at a sufficient distance to prevent overlapping with other plants or overshadowing of the house. There is a tremendous range available, both deciduous and evergreen and offering beauty of blossom, foliage, fruits, bark or a combination of these. With careful choice, they can provide colour and interest throughout the year. Remember to select the kinds which are suitable for your soil and conditions.

Shrubs and a tree or two are vital to any garden. They bring

Opposite: trees and shrubs contribute a variety of colours and shapes to a garden

depth and contrast, supplying a background for other plants, and give welcome shade. Their contribution is lasting and they demand little attention in return, especially if you grow those which need little or no pruning. Although your choice will be largely determined by your own tastes and requirements, spare a thought for your heirs, executors and assigns, as the lawyers call them. What you plant will affect the future value of the property and nothing can more certainly increase it than for estate agents to be able to describe the garden as "mature". (For suitable trees and details of cultivation, see the Wisley handbook, *Trees for small gardens*.)

Screens and hedges

To enclose your garden and perhaps also to divide it internally, some sort of screen is needed. It can be a dead one, such as a fence, or a living one, in the form of a hedge. As far as easy gardening is concerned, the dead boundary has the advantage. A fence needs no clipping or pruning (although a wooden one may require occasional treating with preservative) and it has no roots to rob the border next to it of moisture and nourishment. Your plot probably already has a boundary fence which is perfectly service-able and trouble-free; if you find it unattractive, you can always soften its appearance by training roses, clematis, honeysuckle or other climbers up it.

If you prefer a hedge, for its looks or as a more effective wind-break, you immediately face the problem of fast growth versus slow. You want something that will give you privacy and shelter as soon as possible, but the quicker it grows, the more trimming it will need. One of the fastest evergreen hedges is *Lonicera nitida*, which must be clipped four times a year at the very least. Privet, also rapid-growing, is another that needs several trimmings; it is apt to lose many of its leaves in harsh weather and has notoriously greedy roots. Deciduous hedges have the disadvantage of being bare for much of the year. Hornbeam, however, makes a dense hedge fairly quickly and, like the slower beech, holds its withered russet-coloured leaves during the winter; both require clipping only once a year.

The classic among conifers is the yew, which needs only one trimming a year to make a dense hedge of great quality and dignity; but it is slow and expensive. Cypresses are much faster, although they are best if allowed to develop into tall loose screens without trimming. Otherwise, they should be pruned annually with secateurs. The champion for speed is the hybrid Leyland cypress, which is much planted and much cursed as its tre-

Left: a delightful flowering hedge of currant and forsythia
Right: part of a mixed border, including silvery helichrysum, *Iris pallida* 'Variegata' and ceanothus

mendous rate of rather coarse growth is hard to control. Several cultivars of Lawson cypress make more effective and less troublesome hedges.

For divisions within the garden, where the purpose is mainly ornamental, it is worth considering an informal hedge. Well-known shrubs like forsythia, flowering currant and berberis can be used and usually require only a light prune after flowering.

Herbaceous plants

Herbaceous perennials are the backbone of a garden. They do not normally take long to make mature plants and can then remain in place for several years with little attention except for deadheading and annual tidying up. After two or three years, vigorous plants can be divided and the outer portions replanted separately, discarding the worn-out middle part. The process can be repeated over several years until the border is filled – a leisurely and economical way to garden, which also ensures continuity of display in the long term. Work can be still further reduced by choosing plants which do not need support. If you do have to stake them, this should be done early in the season. The sharp ends of canes or sticks can be dangerous, especially when hidden by foliage, and it is a wise precaution to cover them with plant pots or use hoops or link stakes instead.

With a marked change towards a more natural look in gardens, perennials are no longer confined to the herbaceous border, nor shrubs to the shrubbery. The modern mixed border is essentially labour-saving and brings together a thoroughly democratic assemblage of plants, without any of the old class distinctions that used to exclude some kinds from the company. Herbaceous perennials mingle with shrubs and roses (the latter being less prone to disease than when they were segregated in a separate bed); ferns contribute their special character, as do ornamental grasses and perhaps a bamboo; spring-, summer- and autumn-flowering bulbs find their place in the scheme; and groundcover plants in variety fill in the gaps and create a continuous carpet. Some annuals and biennials may be included to add a splash of colour and even a tender perennial or two could be introduced during the warmer months. These seasonal plantings may make extra work initially, but they are helpful in filling spaces, particularly in the early stages of a border, and can save labour in the end by denying room to weeds. (See also the Wisley handbook, *The mixed border*.)

Vegetables

There is such an abundant supply of excellent vegetables and fruit on sale nowadays that there seems little point in growing your own. Nevertheless, producing food from the garden gives a special satisfaction and no one would dispute that a freshly picked tomato tastes infinitely superior to a shop-bought one. You can also grow a much wider range than might be available in the local greengrocer, including less common vegetables which would otherwise be unaffordable. With a greenhouse or other form of protection, you can even cheat the seasons and raise early lettuces or carrots.

Growing your own is unlikely to save much money and it can involve a lot of hard work if you have a traditional vegetable plot, which must be deeply dug and manured or fertilized each year, quite apart from the business of sowing, planting, weeding, watering and finally harvesting the crop.

This is where perennial vegetables come into their own. One of the best ways to enjoy a taste of luxury in your retirement is to grow asparagus. Although the initial preparation of the bed should not be skimped, it is well worth it as asparagus will go on cropping for years. You will have no trouble with unwanted seedlings if you plant one of the new all-male cultivars, which also give a better yield, and the high shop prices will justify you in claiming that your small indulgence is saving you money.

Another perennial that will provide a touch of extravagance for several years and is easily increased from offsets is the globe artichoke. Given a deeply dug, fertile soil, it can be planted in a border, where it makes a striking feature with its large handsome leaves. To appreciate to the full the subtle flavour of its fleshy thistle-like heads demands a lengthy ritual, which is perfectly suited to the leisurely pace of retirement.

Some annual vegetables, too, would not disgrace the flower bed, notably the unusual Swiss chard or seakale beet, with red or silver tints to the leaves and stems; and that old favourite, the runner bean, which was originally introduced for its flowers and can be trained up a fence.

Tomatoes can be bought at any time of year, but there is nothing to beat the flavour of home-grown ones. They are very easy to grow and thrive in pots or growing bags. 'Sleaford Abundance' is one of the best bush varieties and the exceptionally sweet 'Gardener's Delight' is outstanding among the tall varieties, doing well indoors or out. With lettuce, too, there is no comparison between the average, somewhat elderly, shop-bought article and a freshly cut home-grown one, particularly if it is a choice cultivar such as the compact 'Little Gem'. Some of the non-hearting lettuces, with brown or reddish crinkly leaves, are decorative enough to plant among the flowers.

Lettuces can also be grown in growing bags, perhaps as a second crop after tomatoes, as can several other vegetables such as courgettes, French beans and radishes. Growing bags are a very easy way to cultivate vegetables, ideal where space is limited, but you must ensure that the compost in them does not dry out. They can also be used for exotic vegetables like aubergines and peppers, which need protection, when they may be placed either in the greenhouse or in a sunny sheltered corner of the patio. Growing bags have much to recommend them in the greenhouse, because they save the bother of having to change or sterilize the soil. (For detailed advice on growing vegetables, see The Royal Horticultural Society's *The Vegetable Garden Displayed*.)

Herbs

Freshly gathered herbs have much more flavour than their dried equivalent bought in jars or packets. They will succeed in almost

Above (left): Swiss chard is a most decorative vegetable; (right) tomato 'Gardener's Delight' is highly recommended for flavour and reliability Below (left): chives, parsley, fennel, marjoram and other herbs flourish in a window box; (right) strawberries growing in pots

any type of soil, as well as in pots or window boxes, and most are pretty enough to include in the flower bed – parsley and chervil, for instance, as an edging, thyme spilling over a wall, marjoram as an effective ground cover, rosemary and sage as a low hedge. (For further information, see the Wisley handbook, *Culinary herbs*.)

Fruit

Fruit growing is one of the most fascinating and rewarding branches of gardening, but not one to be undertaken lightly. It demands a great deal of time and labour from the gardener at all times of the year, requires a mastery of specialized techniques and seems to involve a constant battle against pests and diseases.

Probably the fruit that gives the best return for the effort involved is strawberries. These will grow in most soils, if well drained, but should not occupy the same ground for more than three years; after this, rooted runners from the three-year old plants or, preferably, fresh certified stock from a specialist nursery should be planted in a new position. As an alternative to beds, strawberries can be grown in growing bags or in tiers in barrels or special strawberry pots, which has the advantage of keeping the fruits clean and free from slugs and makes them easier to pick. They can also look decorative on a patio. Besides the cultivars that fruit at the ordinary time in early summer, there are others which continue to fruit through the autumn until the frosts.

Currants, both black and red, and gooseberries also produce a good yield relative to the amount of work. All these soft fruits must be netted, or birds will reap the reward for your labours.

Tree fruits need considerably more attention and effort if they are to give satisfactory results. However, you may find it possible to manage apples in restricted forms such as cordons, which require some pruning during the summer, when the weather is kinder, and which make the fruit much easier to reach for picking. Containers also offer scope for growing apples on very dwarf rootstocks, as well as figs and grapes on a sunny and sheltered patio. (For detailed advice, see The Royal Horticultural Society's *The Fruit Garden Displayed* and the Wisley handbook, *Grapes indoors and out*.)

POSTSCRIPT

The sense of smell is said to be the earliest of our senses to develop and the longest to remain with us unimpaired. Even though with the passing years our eyesight may fail, we may still extract undimmed pleasure from the many evocative scents of a garden, particularly one planned with fragrance in mind. (For suitable plants, see the Wisley handbook, *Fragrant and aromatic plants*.)

Nowhere is it more desirable to have scented plants than around that absolutely essential feature of a garden for retirement – a comfortable seat, preferably with some shelter against showers and the glare of the sun, where you can relax. Whether you enjoy good vision or not, or whether you simply want to close your eyes for a quiet snooze, the scents surrounding you will add delight to your rest.

Many lilies have a strong rich scent as well as glorious flowers, which makes them ideal plants for a sitting-out area